READING AND WRITING IN THE MIDDLE GRADES

The Authors

Gary Manning and Maryann Manning are Professors in the School of Education at the University of Alabama at Birmingham. They are also authors of *Improving Spelling in the Middle Grades*; editors of *Whole Language: Beliefs and Practices, K–8*; and coauthors of *Reading and Writing in the Primary Grades*, published by NEA.

Roberta Long is Professor, School of Education, University of Alabama at Birmingham. She is a coauthor of *Reading and Writing in the Primary Grades*.

Advisory Panel

Noreen L. Barney, Third Grade Teacher and Team Leader, Huckleberry Hill School, Brookfield, Connecticut

Katherine Brill, Language Arts Teacher, Krueger Junior High School, Michigan City, Indiana

James Duggins, Professor, Secondary/Post-Secondary Education, San Francisco State University, California

Patricia D. Freeman, Educator, Bartow County, Georgia

Richard Harris, Teacher, Lamar Elementary School, Midland, Texas

Vincent N. Holcomb, Teacher, St. Mary Parish, Louisiana

Joyce Mateicka, Librarian, West Valley Junior High School, Yakima, Washington

Marla M. Streit, Media Center Director, Bourbonnais Upper Grade Center, Illinois

READING AND WRITING IN THE MIDDLE GRADES:
A Whole-Language View

Gary Manning
Maryann Manning
Roberta Long

nea PROFESSIONAL LIBRARY

National Education Association
Washington, D.C.

AUTHORS' NOTE

We have written this publication for teachers of grades four through seven who want to know more about whole-language beliefs and practices We do not ignore theory, but emphasize putting theory into practice. We show how to do this by taking readers into the classrooms of eight model whole-language teachers with whom we have worked closely and over a period of time: Mark Barber, Jody Brewer, Linda Maxwell, Mary-Martha Rhodes, and Jane Weygand of the Homewood (Alabama) City School System; Sonia Carrington of the Vestavia Hills (Alabama) City School System; and Gay Johnson and Cynthia Wisdom of the Birmingham (Alabama) City School System. Although our examples are from the classrooms of these teachers at specific grade levels, the ideas are appropriate for all the middle grades.

AUTHORS' ACKNOWLEDGMENT

We would like to express our appreciation to Delbert Long and Bernice J. Wolfson for their thoughtful suggestions on this manuscript. We are also grateful to Constance Kamii for her contribution to our understanding of constructivism and for her assistance in the development of the model of Language Arts and the Construction of Knowledge.

Printing History
First Printing: January 1990

Note

Library of Congress Cataloging-in-Publication Data

Manning, Gary L.
    Reading and writing in the middle grades   :   a whole-language view /
Gary Manning, Maryann Manning, Roberta Long.
        p.   cm.—(Analysis and action series)
    Includes bibliographical references (p.).
    ISBN 0–8106–3071–0
    1. Reading (Elementary)—United States—Language experience
approach. 2. Language arts (Elementary)—United States.
I. Manning, Maryann Murphy. II. Long, Roberta. III. National
Education Association of the United States. IV. Title. V. Series.
LB1573.33.M36 1990
372.4—dc20   89–29990
                                                                          CIP

CONTENTS

INTRODUCTION

The ideas in this publication are based on (a) the Piagetian theory that knowledge, even social knowledge (including reading and writing), is constructed from within by each individual, and (b) the psycholinguistic view of literacy that learning takes place best when viewed as holistic and when instructional activities and materials for students are authentic and purposeful.

This publication describes our ideas and the ideas of other teachers and researchers who focus on the constructive nature of students' thinking, reading, and writing, and the natural development of these processes. Chapter 1 discusses a model of literacy learning and the role of teachers in creating sound literacy programs for their pupils. Chapters 2 and 3 present instructional ideas that support the literacy development of middle grade students. We include only those ideas that are consistent with what has become known as a whole-language view of literacy development. Goodman et al. (9, p. 6)* describe whole language as "curricula that keep language whole and in the context of its thoughtful use in real situations."

One of the most basic assumptions of whole language provides our theme: reading and writing in school should be natural and enjoyable for students. Teachers can create environments in which students use reading and writing in ways that are authentic. Instead of directing students to complete exercises from a language textbook or to read a story from a basal reader or literature text, teachers can plan so that students learn and use language for real purposes that touch their lives directly. For example, teachers might encourage students to write friendly letters to real people, or to write business letters asking for free materials or inquiring about a topic they are studying. Reading need not take place only in groups, with students reading every story in a basal reader or literature book. Instead, students can read self-selected literature and then have conferences with their teacher or interact with a small group of peers about a book all have read. In other words, reading and writing should occur during the entire day in all content areas; it should not be limited to specific time slots.

---

*Numbers in parentheses appearing in the text refer to the References beginning on page 59.

It is not easy for teachers in the United States today to maintain classrooms that reflect current knowledge of how students develop as thinkers, readers, and writers. The emphasis on skills has had a powerful impact on school curricula. As a result, teachers are pressured to make sure that students master skills and perform well on standardized tests. This, in turn, has led to a fragmented curriculum in which students spend much of their school day practicing skills that are isolated from meaningful contexts. Performance on tests has become the purpose of schooling; schools vie for the "honor" of having the highest test scores.

Teachers try to keep up with the skills checklists in reading and language arts as they document skills taught and "mastered" and as they plow through the tons of ditto paper and workbooks used to teach the skills. It is no wonder, then, that many have come to feel more like file clerks and bookkeepers than teachers.

Nor is life in this kind of classroom pleasant for students. Often they perform tasks that are meaningless to them in order to please the teacher or just to get through the day. They spend much of the school year preparing for state-mandated tests that, in some states, include a nationally standardized achievement test, a state minimum competency test, and a locally developed basic competency test.

Although school life is not bleak for all students and teachers, there are too many joyless and lifeless classrooms where "learning" is pointless and methods of teaching defy what is known about how students learn. When reading and writing are fragmented and isolated from broader contexts, students will not experience language as joyful. For the development of literacy to be enjoyable, students have to engage in real, meaningful, and whole learning experiences. They need access to a wide variety of print materials and time to personally interact with the materials.

There is no set of blueprints for a whole-language classroom. Whole-language teachers create the curriculum in their classrooms based on their personal understanding of theory and research, their own goals and values, and their understanding of how students construct knowledge. Teachers who have been most effective in implementing a whole-language curriculum are those who hold the following beliefs in common:

1. *Students construct their own knowledge from within.* They use their prior knowledge to construct new knowledge. Knowledge is not something poured directly into their heads by some external source. Teachers, therefore, continuously provide opportunities for

students to use knowledge they already have and to take an active role in their own learning.

2. *Literacy activities should be a natural outgrowth of the interests of students.* Instead of engaging in predetermined language arts activities, students select a significant amount of their own reading materials and write about topics of interest to them.

3. *Reading is comprehension—that is, creating meaning from text.* It is not a set of hierarchically arranged subskills to be mastered. The focus of teaching reading is on readers creating meaning as they read. Growth in reading takes place as students read and write whole and meaningful texts.

4. *Communication is the main goal of writing.* Becoming a good writer requires engagement in the process of writing and the support of teachers and peers. Whole-language teachers let students select their own writing topics, accept their attempts to express themselves, and make certain they have an audience for sharing their writing.

5. *Learning to read and write is a social process.* An exchange of points of view contributes significantly to students' construction of knowledge; they think critically when they defend their own ideas and listen to other points of view. Whole-language teachers arrange for students to interact with one another about their reading and writing.

6. *Risk taking and making mistakes are critical to growth in reading and writing.* Making errors is a natural part of learning as students go through various levels of being "wrong." In this way, they construct their own coherent systems of written language. Whole-language teachers encourage students to be autonomous, self-directed learners who view mistakes as a necessary part of learning.

This publication explains the bases of these beliefs and shows how they can provide the foundation for an effective reading and writing program in the middle grades. As a result of such a program, students will become competent readers and writers who find pleasure and satisfaction in reading and writing.

Chapter 1

THE LANGUAGE ARTS AND THE CONSTRUCTION OF KNOWLEDGE

Students construct knowledge of the language arts in the same way they construct knowledge about their world, i.e., they learn by construction from within. According to Piaget, children construct knowledge by modifying their previous ideas (16). In other words, they put new information into relationship with what they already know. The Language Arts and the Construction of Knowledge Model (see Figure 1–1) provides a framework for thinking about how children learn and the central role that the language arts play in the process. The following pages discuss three elements of this model—sources of new information, exchanging points of view, and elaborating and clarifying knowledge through expression and communication.

SOURCES OF NEW INFORMATION

There are many sources of new information; the model shows several, including books, objects, reference materials, and other people. Learners acquire information through experiencing, observing, listening, and reading. During this process, they relate the new information to what they already know about the topic and modify their previous ideas—i.e., they construct knowledge.

EXCHANGING POINTS OF VIEW

Piaget (22) and others (21) show that exchanging points of view contributes significantly to learning; the exchange of ideas stimulates the construction of knowledge. Therefore it is important for students to exchange points of view with others. At the same time, teachers must reduce their adult authority so that when they offer certain ideas students are free to accept or reject them. Many teachers we know encourage their students to interact with one another and proceed with

Figure 1-1. Language Arts and the Construction of Knowledge.

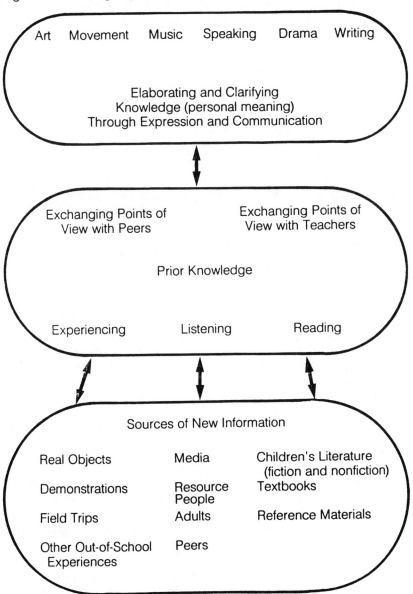

Art   Movement   Music   Speaking   Drama   Writing

Elaborating and Clarifying
Knowledge (personal meaning)
Through Expression and Communication

Exchanging Points of
View with Peers

Exchanging Points of
View with Teachers

Prior Knowledge

Experiencing   Listening   Reading

Sources of New Information

Real Objects   Media   Children's Literature
                                               (fiction and nonfiction)

Demonstrations   Resource   Textbooks
                         People

Field Trips   Adults   Reference Materials

Other Out-of-School   Peers
Experiences

their discussions in a way congruent with Piagetian theory. In a recent visit to a middle-grade classroom, for example, we found students discussing the country's garbage problem, especially as it relates to landfills. When the teacher asked what might happen if there were no more empty landfills, part of the discussion went as follows:

Leonard: Well, just send the garbage to Mississippi.

John: Mississippi doesn't want our garbage.

Leonard: Well, send it to some foreign country.

Niki: Why a foreign country?

Leonard: Because they talk funny and they're dumb.

Justin: They may talk funny but they're smart enough to know garbage when they see it.

Santino: They aren't dumb anyway. They just know different things than we do. And they speak different languages. My uncle lived in Germany.

Leonard: Well, dump it in the ocean.

Mike: We already said the oceans are polluted and the fish are dying.

Leonard: Well, send it to space.

Justin: That doesn't get you anywhere; you're just polluting space.

Mike: There are ways to burn things better so that they don't make too much smoke.

Santino: But it's real expensive and dangerous because you have to heat it up hotter than anything.

The teacher's question stimulated her students to reflect on their personal points of view and make new relationships. She did not intervene with criticism or point out errors in students' thinking. The students were learning with one another as they argued over the landfill issue. Students who feel strongly about their point of view will search for supporting evidence. They will refer to reference materials or other texts. They may interview someone more knowledgeable on the subject. On the other hand, they may change their minds if they feel they are incorrect. As the dialogue about landfills continued for several days, a number of students explored the problem on their own and with peers. One student wrote to several conservation groups and government officials to obtain more information; another interviewed a local government authority. Others read and shared articles from the local newspapers. With the acquisition of more information, the students' prior knowledge of landfills was modified as they related the new material to what they already knew.

ELABORATING AND CLARIFYING KNOWLEDGE THROUGH EXPRESSION AND COMMUNICATION

Students elaborate their knowledge and clarify for themselves what they know as they express their thoughts through writing, speaking, drama, music, art, or movement. When teachers observe these expressions, they can make an evaluation of students' thinking that may be useful for supporting further learning. The students working on landfills decided to make posters illustrating the problems caused by pollution and showing some possible solutions. They also decided to write a play. The teacher asked questions that helped them construct a coherent and orderly account of the knowledge they wanted to share.

We visited the class one day when members of the class shared their information. Some gave research reports, a few shared interviews, others gave their poster reports. We also stayed for the play that was written primarily by Santino and Angel. The scenery, constructed by Justin and Mike, was simple, but detailed enough so that the whole class knew that the setting was an alley by some trash cans with a city skyline as backdrop. The dialogue included some of the same discussion that had taken place earlier in class. The line, "Why don't we send garbage to another state?" had a new twist, however. This time it was Leonard who was convincing the others in a very confident voice that sending the garbage to another state was not a good idea. Through the exchange of viewpoints with others and further study, Leonard realized that his original idea was not a good one. He was thinking for himself as he took several factors about landfills into account and made new relationships.

The play was interrupted several times by the mayor's television appeals to the community to help solve the pollution problem and to try to help stop drug dealers. Even though the play dealt with pollution, it included some action in which citizens told the police not only who the polluters were but also who the drug dealers were. Undercover police officers captured the polluters and drug dealers and uniformed officers

13

dragged the offenders off to jail after a gun battle. Then the mayor thanked the city for its help in the battle against pollution and drugs. The inclusion of drugs in the play did not surprise anyone because of school and community emphasis on this problem.

As students express their thinking, even when they might not be completely on target or correct, they extend and clarify their knowledge. By expressing their ideas through a variety of modes, they develop their ability to think. And this is what whole-language teaching is all about.

In summary, we invite you to think about two of the important ideas reviewed in this chapter: (a) students construct their own knowledge and (b) the language arts play a central role in students' learning. As you read the next two chapters on reading and writing, we trust you will get new information for your teaching and support for what you believe about students' reading and writing development.

Chapter 2

DEVELOPING READERS

Reading has received more attention over a longer period of time than any other area of the curriculum. Federal, state, and local governments have spent significant amounts of money on reading instruction. Nevertheless, there is still an unacceptably high rate of illiteracy in the United States. In addition, there is a high aliteracy rate—i.e., many people who can read do not do so.

There is no common agreement as to the causes of the reading problem and its solutions. We believe that one of the reasons for the high illiteracy rate and the lack of engagement in reading is the overemphasis on testing and the teaching of skills isolated from meaningful context. Too much instructional time is spent taking students through packaged commercial materials to develop skill mastery rather than engaging students in the reading of real texts.

The situation is now changing, however. In many schools, teachers realize that the focus of a reading program should be on comprehension and that readers must engage in reading whole texts, both for information and pleasure. In whole-language classrooms, students read to explore an area of interest or to find information on a topic being studied in class. They read to learn how to construct a volcano or an electromagnet for a science project. They read for the sheer pleasure of it. Meaningful reading occurs throughout the day and across the curriculum.

In order to encourage students to read for enjoyment and to participate in their reading development, whole-language teachers create an environment for reading and teach students strategies to help them achieve these ends. When we walk into Jody Brewer's middle grade classroom, for example, we are excited about the reading community she has created. Jody realizes the importance of giving students time to read books that are of interest to them. She understands the differences and similarities in her students' reading; she recognizes their special interests and allows them to pursue those interests by selecting their own books. At the same time, she knows the importance of reading books by different authors and in different genres; therefore she encourages students to expand their range of selections.

Visitors do not have to ask Jody's students if they like to read; they need only walk into the classroom, observe the students reading, and listen to them talk with Jody and with one another about their reading. These students are enthralled with books. How has Jody created an environment in which students actively engage in reading?

The remainder of this chapter shows how Jody and other whole-language teachers create an educational community that nurtures the development of readers. Their strategies include reading aloud, recorded read-alongs, focus units, choral reading, time for reading, literature sets, reading conferences, book talk, reading journals, book projects, strategy lessons, enlarged texts, cloze procedure, and basal readers.

READING ALOUD

In far too many schools, reading aloud stops at the end of the primary grades. It should be an integral part of the middle grade curriculum as well. Middle graders too enjoy listening to their teacher read aloud. (In fact, as adults we enjoy hearing a good book read aloud. Daily we tune in to public radio to hear that superb reader, Dick Estell.) For many teachers, the favorite part of the school day is reading aloud to students. It is music to a teacher's ear to hear students plead, ''Please read just one more chapter.'' When students are interviewed about favorite books, the ones they mention most often are those their teacher has read to them. An enthusiastic teacher who loves reading to students can cast a spell in a classroom by reading an enjoyable book by a good author. When we find nonbelievers of reading aloud, we invite them to classrooms where we work and let them see for themselves teachers who nurture students' love of reading through the use of this method.

There should be at least one read-aloud time every day. You may want to start the day by reading a poem or a selection from a favorite book. A favorite time for some teachers to read a chapter or two is after lunch. The best time, of course, is when teachers and their students most enjoy it.

There are so many good books to read aloud. Only you can decide which of your favorite stories you will read; your love of the book will shine through to students. You may want to read your favorites to your students year after year; this will make you a better reader of these books. And your students will be the beneficiaries of such a practice.

Sometimes we hear a teacher complain that colleagues at different grade levels read the same book aloud. Interestingly, we never hear students complain about hearing a good book read to them more than once. To avoid repeated use of the same material, however, some schools compile lists of books that teachers at different grade levels read. For a full discussion of reading aloud, *The Read Aloud Handbook* by Trealease (25) will be very helpful. It also provides an excellent annotated bibliography of suggested read-alouds. For a list of new books that are children's favorites, we suggest "Children's Choices," published annually in the October issue of *The Reading Teacher*.

In addition to reading quality fiction, books that are relevant to units of study in the content areas may also be used. Reading aloud can bring some textbooks, as well as nontext sources such as newspapers, magazines, or library books, to life. For example, when studying environmental issues, you may want to read aloud from the classic, *Silent Spring*, by Rachel Carson. Other possibilities include nonfiction and expository texts, biographies, and historical fiction—any kind of book is appropriate if it is related to a particular unit of study in the content areas.

RECORDED READ-ALONGS

Recorded read-alongs should be a part of a middle-grade reading program. Their benefits are similar to those of reading aloud. Listening to recordings of good books, of poems read by outstanding oral readers, or of interviews of politicians or other leaders can be enjoyable and informative to students.

Some teachers use read-along tapes with accompanying texts for content areas. For instance, if a text contains good material that less proficient readers should know about, the teacher makes a tape of that particular section to give those readers access to the information.

FOCUS UNITS: THEME UNITS, AUTHOR AND ILLUSTRATOR STUDIES

A focus unit is centered around literature; it increases students' interest in literature. The focus can be on any literature-related topic, including theme and author/illustrator studies. In a classroom we visit often, the teacher decided to develop a unit around the theme of survival. She collected books on the subject, chose some to read aloud, and made others available to students for their independent reading. In her discussion sessions with students, the teacher helped them understand the similarities between Mafatu from *Call It Courage*, Julie from *Julie of the Wolves*, and Karana from *Island of the Blue Dolphins*. As they discussed the characters in the books they were reading, students' understanding of characterization was extended. They also engaged in a number of activities, including webbing, writing, dramatizing, and participating in readers' theater.

When they focus on the works of an author or illustrator and study biographical information about that person, students develop a personal feeling for the person. Journals such as *Teaching, K-8, Language Arts*, and *Horn Book* provide profiles of authors and illustrators. The following bibliographical sources may also be helpful:

Commire, A. *Something About the Author*. Detroit: Gale, 1971–____. (A set of encyclopedias on children's authors with new volumes added each year.)

Hopkins, L. B. *Books Are by People*. New York: Citation, 1969.

Hopkins, L. B. *More Books by More People*. New York: Citation, 1974.

Kingman, L. *Illustrators of Children's Books*. Boston: Horn Book, 1968, 1977.

Students in Jane Weygand's class recently studied Katherine Paterson. It all began when Jane read aloud *Bridge to Terabithia*. When she finished, the students begged her to read another Paterson story. To show Paterson's range of writing, she chose *The Master Puppeteer*. Then students started reading other works by Paterson, including *The Great Gilly Hopkins* and *Come Sing, Jimmy Jo*. As students looked for more information about the author, Jane shared information about her. Excerpts were read from her *Gates of Excellence: On Reading and Writing Books for Children*. In addition to reading Paterson's books and listening to Jane read aloud, students talked with one another and with her about the books they read; sometimes they read aloud to another person short excerpts from books they found particularly interesting or exciting. As they became more familiar with Paterson's work and gained more information about her, they continued to discuss the author and her books. Building on ideas they gained from *The Master Puppeteer*, they made puppets and became puppeteers. Inspired by the race between Jess and Leslie in *Bridge to Terabithia*, they scheduled a race between the boys and the girls. Because of *Come Sing, Jimmy Jo*, they became intrigued with Appalachian folk music; they listened to it and then sang several of the songs. In fact, they voted to perform for other classes. It was also interesting to see the author's style creep into the writing of some students as they wrote their own stories during writing workshop time.

CHORAL READING, PLAYS, AND READERS' THEATER

Written texts can be shared orally in a variety of ways. Students can do choral readings. They can enact original plays or plays found in books. Many students also enjoy readers' theater.

When we think about choral reading, the image of Betty West, a retired middle-grade teacher, comes to mind. On visits to her classroom, we could feel the pleasure her students derived from their masterful performances as choral readers. During choral reading, the students read either from their own copies or from the overhead transparency their teacher had made. The text came alive as they varied the pitch, inflection, pace, and pauses. Whenever we left Betty's classroom, we had a lingering memory of students enjoying literature as they were developing their abilities and attitudes as readers.

The enactment of plays is another way to enliven literature. Picture books can easily be modified into a script that students can perform. For example, *Amos and Boris* by William Steig (Farrar, Strauss and Giroux, 1971), *The Grouchy Ladybug* by Eric Carle (Crowell, 1977), and *Can I Keep Him?* by Steven Kellogg (Dial, 1971) have enough dialogue that students can adapt into a play format. Other sources for scripts include books, magazines, and basal readers. From our observations, middle graders enjoy dramatizing a book or poem they have read: they also learn a great deal about reading and writing as they enact a script. It is fun to watch students dramatize a familiar story for which they create a new beginning, add new characters, or perform the story from a different point of view.

Readers' theater differs from plays in that there are no costumes, dramatizations, or elaborate sets. Nor do students memorize their lines. The emphasis is on reading the lines of the script, focusing on the meaning of the story. As they read the script, readers make sure that they use appropriate facial expressions and speak in an active voice, appropriately varying the pitch, inflection, and pace. Teachers sometimes help students select literature for readers' theater. The text should have meaningful dialogue and interesting content. Some students rewrite a script to make it more appropriate for this technique. For further information on readers' theater, the following publications will be helpful:

Coger, L. I., and White, M. R. *Readers' Theater Handbook: A Dramatic Approach to Literature*. Glenview, Ill.: Scott, Foresman, 1973.

Sloyer, S. *Readers' Theater: Story Dramatization in the Classroom*. Urbana, Ill.: National Council of Teachers of English, 1982.

TIME FOR READING

Not long ago at the end of a school day, we asked several middle-grade students what they had read during the day. The common response was, "Read? We didn't have time to read." Such a response reflects a school day in which students are too busy with other activities to have time for reading. On the other hand, when we asked students from a whole-language classroom what they had read during the day, we heard a different response. They shared what they had read and at the same time revealed their enthusiasm for reading. In such classes, teachers provide time each day for students to read silently for a sustained period of time; the books they read are those they have chosen. During Jody Brewer's reading instruction time, which consists of a long block of time each day, students engage in silent reading. During that time, however, other activities may include teacher and peer conferences, book projects, and small group interactions formed around literature sets.

LITERATURE SETS

A literature set, simply defined, consists of multiple copies of a book, which enable several students to read the same material at the same time. A small group can be formed in a variety of ways. Sometimes the students themselves decide they will read the same book. At other times, the teacher may assign students or may form the groups in cooperation with the students.

Once a group is set up, with copies of the book, students meet on a regular basis to discuss the book. They soon realize that there are different interpretations for passages and that each reader will often create a slightly different meaning for the same passage. As they interact with one another, their understanding of the book increases. In addition to reading and discussing the work together, students often engage in other related activities. For example, if they are reading *Little House in the Big Woods*, they might also read nonfiction about the settlement of Wisconsin, or other fiction and nonfiction works about the pioneers in middle America. They might also dramatize certain scenes from the book or cook foods that are mentioned in the "Little House" series. As students engage in a variety of activities related to a particular book, their interest in reading is enhanced. Through engagement with books, students truly become readers; they view reading as an integral part of their everyday lives.

READING CONFERENCES

An individual reading conference is an excellent way to promote reading growth. The teacher can use a reading conference to help a reader increase reading interest and comprehension. Following is a conference conducted by Jody Brewer with one of her students, Lauren. They are discussing the story Lauren is reading: *The Wonderful Story of Henry and Six More* by Roald Dahl (Bantam, 1979). (T = Mrs. Brewer; L = Lauren.)

T: Do you think you would like Henry Sugar?

L: Not really, but he gets better toward the end of the story. He gets much better. He devises a system. He read about a guy who could see without his eyes. They wrapped them in a whole lot of bandages but he could still see everything. Henry finally trained himself to do the same thing so he could see what the cards were on the other side and he could win at the casino. I'm not sure how it works.

T: So, he's devised a way to be dishonest and win some more money. Is that right?

L: No, but he's not going to keep it for himself. He's going to make a first class orphanage in every country he goes to. He's not going to be greedy anymore. He get's better in the end.

21

T: So he's sort of like Robin Hood? Robs from the rich and gives to the poor.

L: Yeah, that's exactly right.

T: What would you do if you had all that money?

L: Well, save some for myself and give some to several different things.

T: Do you think you'll finish the book before we talk again?

L: Sure. It's a bunch of different stories and I skip around.

Jody organizes her class so that she has time to confer with every student at least once a week. She closely observes each student, asks questions about what is being read, and offers helpful suggestions. As she conducts conferences, Jody uses a number of options. For example, sometimes she asks a student to read aloud a selection from a text or to retell the story or a part of the story. For more information on reading conferences, see our article, "One-on-One on Reading" (17), *Reading in the Elementary School* by Veatch (27), and *Read On: A Conference Approach to Reading* by Hornsby and Sukarna (15).

PEER READING CONFERENCES

Mary-Martha Rhodes, a middle-grade teacher, emphasizes the importance of peer reading conferences in which students have time to read every day and to talk with her and one another about their books. As peers talk with one another about their reading, their interest and understanding is extended. Mary-Martha's influence upon the interactions between two students, Erin and Brian, is evident in the following peer reading conference about the book, *Ronia, the Robber's Daughter*, by Astrid Lindgren (Viking, 1983).

B: Why did you choose this book?

E: I asked the librarian for a good book. She had two books that she liked but she said this one was really good, so I decided to read it.

B: What has happened so far in this chapter?

E: This girl's father and another robber got into a really bad fight. This girl, Ronia, is trying to keep her friendship with Bart, the other robber's son. She is sort of trying to be smart with him. She talks back to him a lot.

B: Do you know of any other people who would choose this book?

E: Whitney, she might. Mrs. Rhodes might. I don't know of any other people.

B: With this particular book, do you think you should read the first page first or should you read the last page first?

E: Probably start from the beginning.

B: Do you think this is a good book?

E: Yes, it is a very good book. It's interesting and the kind you really want to finish.

B: What was the most interesting part of the book so far?

E: When Ronia meets Birk and they start jumping over this big gap and Birk fell in. What was really interesting was that she didn't like him but she saved his life.

B: Did anyone in your book have a problem?

E: Yes, her father is really overprotective. He came home early just to see her eat dinner.

B: Have you ever had a problem like that?

E: No.

B: What kind of story is this exactly?

E: It is an adventure story. She grows up to be a miniature robber.

B: Does the setting of this story make a difference?

E: I guess so. People don't really live in forests much anymore.

B: Do you think she is a good author?

E: Yes, she is exciting. She makes you want to read more.

BOOK TALK

Book talk fills the air in whole-language classrooms with comments like, "You can't stop reading once you begin to read *Jacob Have I Loved*." Or a student might say to a friend, "It's the kind of book you will like; I know because you liked *Roll of Thunder, Hear My Cry*." A group of girls might be talking about Judy Blume's books. And those who listen to their tone of voice and observe their facial expressions will probably conclude that they are intrigued with Blume's stories.

Book talk occurs spontaneously in classrooms whose teachers have immersed their students in reading. Teachers also organize or formalize book talks. In such cases, students meet in small groups and talk about a book they are reading, asking questions of one another about it. Or in a group of three to five, each student might briefly tell about a book and then answer questions from group members. The teacher periodically meets with the group to model helpful questions and comments.

READING JOURNALS/LOGS

Record-keeping procedures for books students read vary from one class to another. Middle-grade teachers use several methods. For example, the date, the name of the book, and the pages read can be listed as follows:

2-24-89	*The Great Gilly Hopkins*	pp. 1–25
2-26-89	,, ,,	pp. 26–41
2-27-89	,, ,,	pp. 0 (bad day)
2-28-89	,, ,,	pp. 42–52

Or entries in a journal can consist of the name of the book being read, the pages read, and the reader's general impressions:

1-17-89   I went to the library and checked out two Guinness World Record books. I thumbed through one of them.

1-18-89   Yuck! I get tired of people's silly records and I want a real story to read.

1-19-89   I started the first two chapters of *Bright Shadow*. I never heard of the author, Avi. I guess that is his whole name. I like the book.

A third procedure is to list the name of the book being read, record the pages, and give a daily reaction to the text. The following is an example:

4-17-89   I'm reading *Heidi*. I read the first chapter (mostly at home). The book is about a little girl who is sick. She goes to live on this mountain in Switzerland with her grandfather because this lady who took care of her got a new job. The grandpa's name is Uncle Alp and he seems real strange because he is mad at everyone. I guess he was wild and spent his money when he was young.

4-18-89 I read most of the second chapter at school. I had company at home so I couldn't read. This told about a boy named Peter who lived with goats most of the time. Everyday he went to the town and got goats and took them up the mountain for the day. Uncle Alp seems real bad at the first but he turns out to be real nice to Heidi. The lady goes down the mountain and Heidi gets to sleep in the hay.

BOOK PROJECTS

Most students have experienced the age-old practice of doing a book report. Some develop negative feelings about always writing a summary or a critique of the books they read. Instead of writing a book report, we suggest alternative ways for students to respond to their reading. First of all, we prefer to use the term "book projects." This provides a broader framework for responding to books than the traditional written report. While such projects can be useful, they should not be required for every book that students read. Students themselves should decide on the books for which they will develop a project, as well as the form the project will take.

Countless types of projects are possible. We have seen students illustrating a book with pictures, murals, and collages, using a variety of media from clay to paint to transparencies to shredded paper. Some students enjoy writing a script of a portion of a book. Others dramatize a book or a portion of it in an impromptu fashion. And, of course, some students choose to write a formal response to a book that could resemble the traditional book report.

As students engage in these activities, their own understanding of the book can be enhanced. At the same time they are likely to interest others in reading a book they have enjoyed.

STRATEGY LESSONS

A strategy lesson is an instructional activity used to assist readers as they process written language (10). It occurs in the context of reading and focuses on language or thought. Jody Brewer develops strategy lessons based on her observations of what readers need to help them become more proficient. For example, if a student is not constructing meaning when reading, she suggests alternative strategies such as rereading or reading ahead. Or she uses contextual clues, individual conferences, the cloze procedure, and prediction strategies, as illustrated in the following pages.

When a reader doesn't know a word in a text, Jody helps him/her develop meaning through context by using a suggestion of Goodman and Burke (10). She asks the student to first decide if knowing the word is necessary in order to make sense of the text. If not, the student continues reading. If the reader decides it is necessary to know the word, Jody then encourages him/her to predict what the word means, based on everything learned in the story and the reader's prior knowledge. Each time a reader comes up with a possible word, Jody asks if it makes sense in the context of the sentence. If it does not make sense, she encourages him/her to continue searching for a word that does.

As a teacher, Jody's responsibility is to know what students are doing as they read and to provide instruction to help them become better readers. This instruction takes place in an individual conference, in a small group that is invited together for a specific purpose, or in a whole-class situation. Through skillful questioning in individual reading conferences, Jody helps readers become more proficient. For instance, an examination of some of the questions Jody asks Lauren in the transcription of their reading conference (see Reading Conferences, pp. 21–22) shows that she is helping Lauren with characterization. When she asks Lauren if she thinks she would like to know Henry Sugar, this causes Lauren to reflect on the character. Together teacher and student compare Henry Sugar with Robin Hood. As Jody continues to help Lauren gain insights about characterization through such questioning, Lauren's understanding of the ways authors reveal characters is deepened. Jody might also use other activities. She might suggest that Lauren write a story in which Henry and Robin Hood carry on a conversation. Or Lauren and other students who are reading Dahl books could meet in a small group to compare and contrast the major characters in such books as *The Wonderful Story of Henry and Six More, James and the Giant Peach,* and *Charlie and the Chocolate Factory.* They might also find examples of different ways Dahl reveals his characters.

Jody recently created several passages for a student who was regularly reversing the words "where" and "were." Using passages in which "where" occurred frequently, she deleted it each time it occurred, making certain that "were" would not make sense. When the student read the passages, she wanted him to experience disconfirmation if he used "were" rather than "where"; this should help him focus more on meaning cues and less on sound-symbol cues when reading. (Also see Cloze Procedure, p. 28.)

Jody also reads aloud to her students each day. During a recent read aloud of *James and the Giant Peach*, she had just finished reading about James and the insects on the giant peach with the sharks nibbling at the peach. At that point, she asked students to predict what would happen to James. One student said, "I don't know how, but he will escape—the sharks won't get him." Another student said, "I think a sea gull will rescue him." Others offered their predictions. After Jody read the next section, one student said, "I was almost right, but not quite—it took more seagulls than I thought." As students compared and contrasted their ideas with the actual story, they confirmed or revised their original predictions. Through this and similar instructional activities, Jody is helping her pupils develop prediction strategies that should improve their reading and listening comprehension. Prediction strategies require students to use prior knowledge that is relevant to a story; they strive to match their expectations with the meaning intended by the author.

ENLARGED TEXTS

Enlarged texts or big books are usually found in primary grade classrooms, but they also have value in the middle grades. In fact, we use enlarged texts with adults. For example, if we want everyone to read a portion of a text, silently or in unison, we put it on a transparency for use on an overhead. In that way everyone is able to focus on the same information at the same time.

Big books with nonproficient middle-grade readers can be used in a way similar to their use with younger students. The content of the text, however, must be suitable for middle graders. Teachers read the enlarged text aloud, perhaps pointing to the words as they read, but they are careful to read the whole text naturally and not to dwell on individual words or sentences. A first reading of the entire text may be followed by having students read along with the teacher on repeated readings. Teachers may also focus on certain features of the text. As teacher and students participate in the shared reading experiences with the enlarged text, students may learn several literary and linguistic factors described by Holdaway (14): the syntax of language, vocabulary development (by hearing words not used in their normal conversation), intonation patterns, in which listeners hear new literacy patterns that vary from conversation, and idioms that use special forms different from normal grammatical or syntactic rules.

CLOZE PROCEDURE

A cloze procedure is the systematic deletion of words from a written text that can be used as a teaching technique. The teacher selects a passage and deletes every nth word. The deletions might be made randomly or systematically, such as every other adjective if the teacher wants to focus students' attention on adjectives. Students are then asked to determine the words that would make sense in the blank spaces. Emphasis should be given to getting students to select words that make sense to them and that at the same time keep the intended meaning of the author. We suggest having students work in pairs or in small groups to complete cloze exercises because they will benefit from interaction with others. The following exercise is from an excellent book on the subject, *Cloze Procedure and the Teaching of Reading* by Rye (24, p. 57):

> The teacher can help the _____ process continue after the _____ by giving credit for appropriate, as well as correct responses, and by explaining possible _____ behind the author's choice of words.

We deleted the following words: *learning, discussion, reasons.* In a workshop session, we would give this passage to participants and ask them to move into small groups to discuss and agree upon the words they think we deleted. Then, we would ask participants to give reasons for their choices that might cause them to reflect more deeply on the passage.

BASAL READERS

Basal readers should be used as only one of many types of reading material. It is important for teachers to realize that many of the selections are modified versions of stories by well-known authors, which are not as interesting or as well-written as the originals.

We suggest that the stories in the basal reader should not be read in sequence but that students select those that are of interest to them. Of course, at times the teacher may suggest that a student read a certain story. Jane Weygand did this when a student reading mysteries was trying to write one of his own but was having difficulty structuring his story. Jane referred him to a basal reader mystery that had accompanying clues. As teacher and student read and discussed the story, the boy became more knowledgeable about structuring a mystery and this helped him become a budding mystery writer.

In other classrooms we know, when a few students decide to read the same story from a basal reader, they follow a procedure similar to the one we suggested for literature sets. A group of students who want to participate in readers' theater might find a story in a basal reader that serves their purpose. In other words, whole-language teachers may use selections from basal readers, but they and their students use them selectively. In addition, teachers may refer to the teacher's manual and use those suggestions that are congruent with whole-language beliefs. For example, basal readers usually provide bibliographies of books that center around a certain theme or unit of study and include suggestions for book-extending activities.

ASSESSING DEVELOPMENT OF READERS

To determine how students are developing as readers, the teacher has to assess what meaning they are creating as they read. One way to do this is to ask a student to read a story and then to retell it. We suggest an unaided and aided retelling procedure, developed by Goodman, Watson, and Burke (11), in which the teacher asks the reader to retell the story and follows the retelling with more specific questions about what the student has related. If the reader retells the text with most of its meaning, the teacher knows he/she understands the story.

Miscue analysis is another assessment procedure that is most helpful. A miscue is an unexpected response in oral reading. For instance, if you read the previous sentence aloud, reading "writing" rather than "reading," you made a miscue. An analysis of readers' miscues shows their strengths as well as their problems. To use miscue analysis with readers who are having difficulty, we suggest Goodman, Watson, and Burke's *Reading Miscue Inventory* (11). In most cases with typical readers, you need only note miscues to determine if there is a change in meaning. When you listen to a student read orally, ask yourself this question: Does the sentence make sense with the miscue? If it does, the reader is probably focused on meaning and there is no cause for concern since all readers make such miscues. For example, if a student reads, "The *pony* was running down the hill,'' rather than, ''The *horse* was running down the hill,'' the sentence makes sense with the miscue. But if a student reads, ''The *house* was running down the hill,'' the sentence does not make sense. If the reader's miscues do change the meaning, there is a need for the student to become more focused on meaning.

Another helpful way to assess individual reading growth is to keep a record of the reading completed by a student. Reading journals or logs, discussed earlier in this chapter, should provide useful assessment information for the teacher. Brief anecdotal comments may be included on the record kept by the teacher.

When teachers carefully observe students, they draw significant conclusions about reading habits, and find answers to important assessment questions: Does the student choose reading from among different options in the classroom? Is the student reluctant or enthusiastic when there are opportunities to select books from the classroom or central library? Does the student participate in shared literature experiences?

We are especially opposed to relying heavily on formal assessment procedures to judge a student's reading ability, particularly those procedures that purport to measure reading isolated from meaningful text. Most standardized and criterion-referenced tests use only word parts, words in isolation, single sentences, or short paragraphs to assess reading ability. This type of evaluation reflects a belief that reading can be reduced to isolated skills; it ignores the fact that reading is a process of creating meaning from written text.

Reading tests built on a segmental view of reading do not measure a student's actual reading ability. Therefore, we suggest using the informal methods suggested in this section. In addition, some published informal reading inventories can be helpful if they focus on assessing readers' comprehension of whole pieces of text rather than merely counting the number of errors the reader makes. Finally, it is important that teachers keep a folder documenting each student's reading growth and use this record as a basis for planning appropriate learning activities.

Chapter 3

DEVELOPING WRITERS

Writing has always been one of the basics of American education. Until recently, however, it was primarily "creative" writing, consisting of teacher-assigned topics or sentence starters. Usually it took place only once a week; Friday seemed to be the most popular day for this assignment. Grammar, punctuation, and spelling were taught as separate entities in the belief that they would help students become better writers. Teachers used their trusty red pencils to show how much they knew that their students did not know about language.

Thanks to such dedicated researchers as Calkins (3) and Graves (12), and to an expanded knowledge of how children learn, we now know that this is not the best way to teach writing. In a whole-language classroom, teachers and students write frequently and for many purposes throughout the school day. Students keep journals to document their learning in subject areas. They write letters to order supplies or to obtain information about a topic they are studying. They send invitations and thank-you notes. Every day there is a block of time for writing workshop. During this time everyone writes on self-selected topics of interest. Teacher and students exchange ideas as they work together to develop a text. Through whole-class or small-group minilessons, the teacher provides instruction and confers with individual students about their writing. As students engage in the writing process, they develop their skills and learn about the technical aspects of writing.

This chapter first describes middle grade writers and then discusses ideas that are appropriate for a whole-language classroom. It discusses the writing process and how this process is fostered through the writing workshop and through writing activities outside the writing workshop. It emphasizes the importance of the teacher as a model and the importance of students interacting with the teacher and with one another as they engage in writing activities.

Through the research of Graves (12) and others, we know that all students can write and that most want to write. Middle grade writers differ greatly, though, in the writing strengths and interests they bring to the classroom. They differ in their ability to focus a piece of writing, to gain control over a point of view in their writing, and to begin a story and carry it through to the middle and the end. They also differ in their knowledge and use of the conventions of written language.

By the middle grades, some students have developed extraordinary abilities to write in a specific genre such as poetry or nonfiction prose. Some are best at developing stories based on personal experiences; others use their imagination and knowledge of the world and literature to create stories of fantasy or even science fiction. Teachers need to know the strengths that students bring to the classroom and focus on those strengths to help them continue to develop as writers.

Middle grade students are diverse in their writing interests. We recently reviewed the writing folders in Sonia Carrington's class and were amazed at the variety of topics the students had selected to explore. All of Carol's stories were about European royalty; Willard wrote mostly mysteries. Two students had pieces on space exploration and several had written earthly adventure stories. A large number of stories were about personal and family experiences. Susan focused on poetry about oceans and beaches. We were especially impressed with two nonfiction reports, one on blindness and another on the naval academy. Sonia's students select their own topics for writing; the quantity and quality of the written work in this classroom far exceeds that found in a classroom where the teacher assigns the topic or gives story starters. Whole-language teachers capitalize on the interests of their students and know when and how to help them expand their interests as they engage in different forms of writing.

In whole-language classrooms, daily writing is an expectation and a vital part of the school day. Teachers cannot force students to want to write, but their desire to write is enhanced when they are actively engaged in the process of writing and they experience success and improvement as they write about things they know and that are of interest to them. Just ask a student in a writing process classroom, "Do you like to write?" You are likely to get the answer we got recently: "Like it! No, I love it!"

As you read the ideas presented in the following pages, we hope you will find them useful in creating meaningful writing in your classroom. We want the teaching of writing to be as satisfying for you as it is for the teachers mentioned here.

WRITING WORKSHOP

Writing workshop gives students an opportunity to engage in the writing process. According to Calkins (3), the writing process consists of rehearsal, drafting, revision, and editing. These processes are, of course, not linear; they are recursive and they overlap. In fact, as we drafted this section for the nth time, we continued to rehearse and edit. As we prepared to write this book on reading and writing in the middle grades, we rehearsed. Our rehearsal occurred in several ways: observing many process classrooms, interacting with teachers and students in those classes, reading books and articles on process reading and writing, and interacting on a personal basis with Ken and Yetta Goodman, Dorothy Watson, and Lucy Calkins. When we started, the early drafts were quite bad, but as we revised, we began to express our ideas more clearly.

Graves (12) and Calkins (3) recommend that teachers provide an hour each day for students to engage in the writing process. Several components comprise the writing workshop: modeled writing, minilessons, teacher and peer conferences, sharing time, and publishing.

Jane Weygand conducts a writing workshop each day for an hour. During the first few minutes, she may conduct a minilesson or she may model her own writing for students. When she models, she usually writes on the overhead and talks with students about her writing as she composes. During most of the workshop time, students engage in writing, but they may confer with Jane or a peer. In fact, Jane schedules writing conferences with one-fifth of her students each day, which means that she conferences with every student in her class at least once a week. In addition, she reserves some time each class period for students who need a conference before their scheduled conference time. The last few minutes of writing workshop are reserved for sharing time.

Each of Jane's students has two folders for his/her writing; these folders are kept in a central place in the classroom. One of the folders contains all the first draft writing the student has completed; Jane calls this an inactive file. The other folder, the active file, contains the piece the student is currently writing.

The following discussion elaborates on several aspects of the writing workshop—modeling, minilessons, teacher and peer conferences, sharing time, publishing, and the use of language arts textbooks.

Modeled Writing

Modeling is an important condition for learning to write, or, for that matter, for learning almost anything. Just as learning to drive a car can be facilitated by observing other people driving cars, so can teachers help students learn to write well by modeling for them the act of writing. At one point the writing process in Linda Maxwell's classroom was not going well. After reflecting on her writing workshop and concluding that she needed to model for her students, she composed a story on the overhead and talked through some of the writing process as she composed. It worked! You can imagine her excitement when students responded eagerly to her writing, offered comments, and asked questions of her as a writer. More importantly, they had a renewed interest in their own writing. Needless to say, modeling became an integral and important part of Linda's writing workshop.

Minilessons

Minilessons are short instructional lessons (as little as two minutes and usually no more than ten minutes) on a specific topic (3). They can be on any aspect of writing from topic selection to paragraph development. Recently we observed Mark Barber conducting a minilesson on how to show and not just tell, using ideas from *Write to Learn* by Murray (19). The following is an example he developed:

Telling: I like to roller skate.

Showing: Every Saturday I skate at Rollerland. Whirling around
           the rink on my new skates and feeling the rush of air
           splash against my face makes me feel as fresh as a
           new-born chick. I'm a ballet dancer as I twirl and whirl
           across my make-believe stage.

In a visit to Sonia Carrington's classroom, we found her conducting a minilesson on sources of information, one of several lessons she had planned on different aspects of writing research reports. Her plan for the next several days included lessons on recording bibliographical information, note taking, outlining, and drafting the report using notes.

Teacher and Peer Conferences

Teacher and peer conferences can help students think critically and independently. In a conference, the teacher must be a sensitive listener and skillful questioner, which, in turn, will help students become sensitive listeners and skillful questioners in their peer conferences. Questions such as the following can help writers think more clearly about what they have written:

- What else could you say about what you have written here?
- When you told me about your accident, there were lots of details, but you haven't written very many of those details. Would you like to add anything?
- Are you satisfied with this section?

In conducting a writing conference, the teacher has an opportunity to help the writer consider what has been written and think of ways to expand or improve the piece. This is best done by focusing on the meaning and clarity of the story rather than on the mechanics of writing.

Another benefit of the writing conference is that students begin to model the same behaviors and questions that the teacher demonstrates. They read or listen to each other's work for appreciation and to raise questions for clarification or to make suggestions for improvement. They support and help each other. An example of such support occurred on one of our visits to Linda Maxwell's class. Two students were huddled together in the corner of the room. As we listened we heard them drafting and revising several beginnings to one student's piece. Linda told us that a student who was excellent at drafting good beginnings was helping the other get started.

Most teachers improve their writing conferencing techniques with experience. As they model improved techniques for their students, peer conferences occurring in the room will improve also. There is no one "right way" to conduct a conference. Some students are sensitive and must be treated carefully; others readily consider suggestions about ways to improve their writing. Without question, however, writing conferences—like reading conferences—are well worth the time and effort.

Sharing Time

At the end of each writing workshop, students share their writing. The time may vary but it usually lasts about ten minutes. The sharing sessions can be organized in different ways. Students may sign up on a voluntary basis or they can be scheduled to share on certain days; everyone should have an opportunity to share at least once a week. During share time, a student might read an entire piece or only a portion of it. It may be a finished piece or a work in progress. By sharing, students get feedback from teacher and classmates on ways to improve the text. Teachers also may take the "author's chair" (see Graves and Hansen [13]) and ask for suggestions on their writing or reactions to a completed piece. On a visit to Linda Maxwell's writing workshop, she was sharing a piece she had written. She read her story and then asked her students, "What do you like about what I have written?" When they finished offering comments, she asked, "What questions do you have about what I have written?" After listening to the questions, Linda said she would consider them in her next draft. By writing with her students and sharing her writing with them, Linda demonstrates that she is a writer and is a part of their writing community.

Publishing

Publishing or celebrating authorship can occur in a number of ways. Gay Johnson uses several forms of publishing. For instance, students develop posters and invitations; they write letters to friends, family, and others, as well as articles for the class newspaper. Gay also requires students to publish at least one individual book every six weeks. The publishing procedures vary from one six-week period to another, but she encourages them to use a sturdy cover and bind the cover and pages in a durable way.

Gay realizes that publishing is the end of a long process of rehearsing, drafting, revising, and editing. After the students themselves have edited the work they have chosen to publish and have also edited it with a friend, Gay serves as the final editor. Publishing requires a great deal of effort and time for a teacher, but it is well worth it. Gay's reasons for making publishing an essential ingredient of her writing workshop echo those given by Graves (12): it contributes to students' writing development; it helps them gain a sense of audience as they realize that what they write will be read by other people; it gives them a sense of accomplishment that can be further realized as parents take pride in their children's finished products; and it gives the teacher an opportunity to work with students in meaningful ways to improve their spelling, punctuation, and other surface features of their writing.

In addition to sharing their published writing in the classroom and the school, Gay provides opportunities for students to share their work with others outside the school. For instance, each year her students, along with over 2,500 other students from kindergarten to eighth grade, participate in the annual Young Authors' Conference held at the University of Alabama at Birmingham. At that conference, students have an opportunity to listen to well-known authors, participate in book-related activities, and share with one another their published works. Gay also encourages her students to submit their polished pieces to publishers who will print students' original works (see Appendix A).

Language Arts Textbooks

Many of the whole-language teachers we know refer to English textbooks, but they are not driven by them. For example, Linda Maxwell and her students refer to the textbook and other resources when they need to know something and they feel the text can be of help. Linda sometimes uses ideas from the text for a minilesson in her writing workshop or to help a student with a strategy during a writing conference. She and other whole-language teachers with whom we work find little, if any, reason to use a workbook or practice materials that accompany the textbooks. These materials tend to be skill-based, consisting of isolated and fragmented exercises. In the writing workshop and in writing activities outside the workshop, students develop the strategies they need in the process of writing, not by proceeding in a sequential order through a textbook.

WRITING OUTSIDE THE WORKSHOP

Writing is a powerful tool for thinking and learning; it should not be limited in the classroom to the writing workshop. Students should have many opportunities throughout the school day to engage in writing. By incorporating writing in all curriculum areas throughout the day, students' writing abilities will improve. The major purpose for incorporating writing in various curriculum areas, however, is to help students clarify and extend their knowledge in specific areas. This section discusses several ideas for emphasizing writing throughout the day—journal writing, written conversations, research projects, and letter writing.

Journal Writing

Journal writing is an important activity in middle grade classrooms. Not only do students enjoy writing in a journal where they have the opportunity to write freely without fear of teacher correction, but journals provide a means for clarifying and extending knowledge. The journal can be used to record thoughts of a personal nature or ideas dealing with a particular content area. Entries are usually made in a spiral notebook or in a notebook consisting of several sheets of paper stapled together.

Personal journals are used by students to record their thoughts. The following is an example of a personal journal entry by a middle grade student:

> Today is Cahalans birthday! she brought a cake to school. We will have to have our teeth checked sometime today, probably! Last weekend I brought home my practice book and my wrighting foulder an I forgot them and the practice books are due tomorrow and tomorrow is the last day we will write in our writing foulders.

Students usually make an entry in their journals at a specific time set aside each day for journal writing; they are encouraged by the teacher to write on anything they wish. Journals may be stored in a certain place in the classroom or kept in students' desks. Most teachers look at the journals on a rotating basis, reading those of five or six students each day so that by the end of the week they will have read the entries of all their students.

Some teachers occasionally respond in writing to the entries with such comments as, "I really enjoyed reading about your trip," or "Tell me more about your new computer game." A few teachers engage in what is known as dialogue journals, carrying on a written conversation with students. Dialogue journals provide an excellent way for frequent, personal, and meaningful communication between teacher and student.

Content journals provide a way for students to review or interpret information discussed in class or read in a text. A content journal is one of the most effective strategies for incorporating writing in the content areas (7, 18, 26). Mary-Martha Rhodes varies the type of entries she asks students to make. For example, she might ask students to respond to specific questions such as, What did you learn? What would you like to know that wasn't discussed in class today?

James wrote the following response to these questions in his science journal:

> We are learning about different kinds of energy, namely chemical, heat, sound, light, mechanic, and electric. Kinetic energy is the energy

of motion. Potential energy is stored energy. There seem to be six types or forms of energy that we learned about.

I would like to know more about mechanic energy. I think it would be interesting.

At other times, Mary-Martha does not ask specific questions; she simply asks students to write something about a particular subject at the end of the class period. In a social studies class, Susan wrote the following:

I feel good after doing my project. It showed me nothing is impossible. At first I thought it was going to be a disaster but with a little skill it was done. I don't know if it will be good enough.

Jonathan made the following entry in his science journal:

Science is neat. I love this chapter. I hope I do good on the test. I wish we could do some more of the experements.

Dialogue journals are time-consuming, but well worth the effort; they enable teachers to communicate with students. Sonia Carrington follows procedures given by Atwell (2) as she corresponds with her students about books they are reading. The following is an example of a written dialogue between Sonia and Meredith:

9–7–89

Dear Mrs. Carrington,

I'm reading *Anne of Green Gables* and it's fabulos. It's so descriptive. I love the characters. I love how Anne imagines so much and in a way I think I'm a little like her because she's talkative, fun, and sweet. One thing I don't like about her is that she asks to many questions. Well, I'll get back to you.

Meredith

9–8–89

Dear Meredith,

I haven't read *Anne of Green Gables*, but you have aroused my curiosity. When I read it, I'll let you know how I like it.

Mrs. Carrington

9-20-89

Dear Mrs. Carrington,

I've finished *Anne of Green Gables* and I loved the book so much. Some people say the book is better than the movie. I agree. It's going to be hard choosing another book from the awesome selection. I might get *Bunnicula* because I've heard it was so funny and mysterious. I think I'm going to have fun doing the fiction booklet. If you have any other suggestions on books that might be good for me, pleas tell me. Thank you.

Meredith

9-25-89

Dear Meredith,

Books are usually better than movies, I think. You can visualize everything in your own mind. Oh, yes, *Bunnicula* is a fun book. The animals' lives are such a mystery, especially Bunnicula's. And Harold turns out to be such a good friend. Tell me what you think about it when you finish it. I'm so pleased, Meredith, that you like to read. Every time I glance your way you have your nose in a book—how wonderful!

Mrs. Carrington

Written Conversations

In the dialogue and response journals described above, both teachers and students interact in writing. In fact, the teacher is carrying on a written conversation with students. Another method of clarifying and extending learning is for students to respond to other students in writing.

We use written conversations with students in our graduate courses. We ask students, working in pairs, to ask their partners to write a comment or a question about the class discussion or reading. The writer then hands the paper to the partner who responds in writing to the question or comment. This process continues for a given period of time. Most often, we begin by asking both partners to initiate the writing and then exchange papers as they respond to each other in writing. By using two papers rather than one, both partners are engaged in writing at the same time, rather than one remaining inactive while the other is responding to questions or comments.

In addition to using written conversations with the entire class to help students explore a topic of study, some teachers encourage students to use written conversations when they wish to converse with a partner, perhaps about a book both are reading. And students working on a project in small groups can use written conversations to avoid disturbing others who may be engaged in quiet study.

Research Projects

In the introduction to this chapter, we mentioned that we were impressed with two nonfiction reports written by Sonia's students. One of these was on the U.S. Naval Academy. When we talked with Jeremy, the author of the report, he explained that he had become interested in the naval academy because of his friendship with his next-door neighbor, Captain Florence, a retired naval officer and a graduate of Annapolis. After Jeremy selected his topic, he began to read about the academy from a variety of sources in the school and the public library and in publications from the naval office. He also interviewed Captain Florence who proved to be a valuable resource. During his reading and interviewing, Jeremy took careful notes. He even audiotaped his conversations with Captain Florence and then transcribed them. After his research, he began to write. Following the advice of his teacher, he did not refer to his notes as he drafted. After completing his first draft, he compared it with his notes, inserting and deleting information. Then, after conferring with one of his friends, he made further revisions based on the friend's comments and questions. During the course of his drafting, he also conferred with his teacher and then shared his draft with Captain Florence who worked with him on further revision. When he was satisfied with the content of the report, he began to edit. He also asked a friend and the teacher to edit. When he discussed the published report with us, he beamed. Jeremy had accomplished what Calkins (3) recommends: he had written a nonfiction text with voice and energy.

Letter Writing

Most teachers incorporate letter writing in their language arts curriculum, as it is addressed in most language arts textbooks. However, because it tends to be an exercise in learning how to write letters, the student often sees no real purpose for the activity other than to complete the assignment. But if students have a real purpose for writing letters, the experience can be enjoyable and useful.

41

It is satisfying to students to get a response from a letter they have written to businesses or government offices. We have observed their enthusiasm when they receive a reply to a letter they have written to a favorite author. For several excellent suggestions on letter writing, we recommend *P.S. Write Soon*, which was produced by the U.S. Postal Service in cooperation with the National Council of Teachers of English (1111 Kenyon Road, Urbana, IL 61801).

ASSESSMENT OF WRITING

A major reason for assessing writing is to help teachers teach better and to help writers write better. Assessment should be regarded as a teaching and learning tool rather than simply as a tool for measuring products.

Process writing teachers are confronted with a number of dilemmas in writing assessment. For example, their students have to take a standardized achievement test which consists of a language portion that usually measures language usage and writing mechanics rather than the ability to compose. While this is a real concern to writing process teachers, we are finding that middle-level students in writing process classrooms perform on this test as well as if not better than do students in traditional language arts classrooms. For instance, last year Linda Maxwell's students' scores on the language portion of a standardized achievement test were higher than the scores of students in traditional classrooms in comparable schools.

Asking students to write on a particular topic in a test situation for a limited period of time is another poor assessment procedure that now confronts writing process teachers. The student's writing ability is assessed by using one writing sample. Needless to say, such a procedure is unfair to the writer and to the writer's teacher. Indeed, the writing quality of even very skillful writers varies from day to day and could well be judged unskillful if they were asked to write in a test situation on a given day. If this type of formal assessment is required, teachers need to lobby for students to be allowed to write on a topic of their choice and to be given the opportunity to revise and redraft the piece. If formal assessment is required by the school system, teachers should have the flexibility to ask each student to select a piece of writing that has been revised, developed, and edited through several drafts, and that reflects his/her writing talents. That piece would then be submitted for assessment.

When evaluation is based on a single writing sample written in a test-like situation, only the product of the student's writing is being assessed. In such cases, many educators recommend a holistic scoring procedure whereby the whole piece of writing is assessed, with emphasis on content rather than on mechanics. For more information on assessment and evaluation of writing, we refer readers to other publications such as *Measures for Research and Evaluation in the English Language Arts* (6) and *A Procedure for Writing Assessment and Holistic Scoring* (20).

Writing process teachers assess writers as they confer with them, as they observe them conferring with one another, and as they observe them in the process of writing. When teachers listen to students share their drafts, they respond to them in ways that should further writing development. To assess students' writing development over a long period of time, teachers can use a variety of record-keeping procedures. For example, they can use checklists with spaces for comments to record information about items they consider important in writing: (a) attitude toward writing, (b) topic selection, (c) fluency in first drafts, (d) adequate information in drafts, (e) clarity and precision of expression, (f) sequence of information, (g) beginnings and endings of drafts, (h) use of vocabulary, (i) sentence structure, (j) use of paragraphs, and (k) mechanics and spelling. Teachers may also want to include various other features of writing such as unique voice of the writer.

Keeping writing samples in folders provides another excellent resource for teachers to assess the development of their students. This can be the simplest and most significant of all procedures used to assess a writer's development over a given period of time. Just recently, a parent visiting a writing process classroom teacher was concerned about the boy's development as a writer; she thought he was not making adequate progress. The teacher welcomed the parent, said that she, too, wanted the student to develop as a writer, and suggested that they examine his writing kept in a folder. Placing samples of the student's writing, from the beginning of the year to the present, side by side on a table in the room, the teacher read and studied the papers with the parent. In this way, both could see the progress of the writer. Following the review, the mother said, "I forgot where my child was at the beginning of the year; I'm amazed at his progress." Indeed, the teacher and the mother could see for themselves the tremendous progress the boy had made as a writer.

In addition to nonpublished work in the folders, the actual published work of students provides an excellent way to assess their writing devel-

Chapter 4

FINAL COMMENTS AND QUESTIONS

This publication began with a statement of several beliefs usually held in common by whole-language teachers: knowledge is constructed from within; literacy activities should be a natural outgrowth of the interests of students; reading is comprehending; communicating is the main aim of writing; reading and writing are social processes; taking risks and making mistakes are essential to growth. The chapters that followed provided additional insights about the language arts as well as ideas congruent with whole-language theory.

The implementation of a whole-language curriculum in your classroom may not be easy if you are required to follow rigid guidelines imposed by the school district, the state department of education, and/or other external groups. These guidelines are usually lists of skills isolated from meaningful context and are touted as the way to achieve "excellence." In our view, they have decreased "excellence" as students are often busy completing skills exercises rather than reading whole texts that are interesting to them and writing texts in which they effectively express their ideas.

Sensitive teachers realize the pitfalls of following a predetermined curriculum. Many have observed for themselves the uninterested and detached learners in classrooms. They confirm what Goodlad (8, p. 112) discovered in his landmark study: "Classes in our sample at all levels tend not to be marked with exuberance, joy, laughter, abrasiveness, praise..." He further observed that there is a relatively flat emotional tone, especially in upper elementary and secondary classrooms. When teachers follow a predetermined language arts curriculum by plodding through English texts, literature texts, and basal readers, students often find it difficult to become interested in and excited about what they are learning. Teachers, too, find little personal meaning in a predetermined curriculum. One such teacher told us, "I am an avid reader and the boredom I offered my students and myself in the name of reading instruction upset me greatly. I vowed I would change." And she did.

Goodlad's findings would be different if he and his researchers were to visit her present classroom and the classrooms of other whole-language teachers; they would see teachers and students personally involved in their reading and writing, following no prescribed curriculum guides or canned lessons. These teachers realize the need to move away from the control of outside mandates, lockstep processing of textbooks, and the emphasis on tests. They are using strategies and materials that help them create a learning environment where students are empowered to think and to effectively use oral and written language. They demonstrate the value of such teaching and work with other teachers to better understand students' language learning and the conditions necessary to support it.

As teachers become interested in whole language, they reflect on their own beliefs about language learning and the practices they use to help their students become increasingly literate. Teachers and students not only read and write with one another, they also talk about their reading and writing. And they make new discoveries about books, themselves, and one another. The atmosphere is filled with enthusiasm and excitement. Only a sensitive teacher working with particular students is in a position to develop such a language arts program. We hope all of our readers can receive enough of the needed respect, support, and trust from the administration, colleagues, and parents so that they and their students experience the joys of teaching and learning. Unfortunately, however, some whole-language teachers work in schools where they are required to use basic texts and traditional teaching methods.

What can whole-language teachers do who are required to use basic texts and traditional teaching methods?

Whole language is not a specific method or a set of materials; rather it is a set of beliefs about language learning. Whole-language teachers believe in children and their power to learn when what they are learning makes sense to them in their world. If required to use basic texts and traditional methods, teachers find it difficult to keep reading whole and meaningful for their students. Teachers with a whole-language view, however, find ways of minimizing the time and effort students spend on the required texts. They attend to only those suggestions in the teacher's manual that are consistent with their views. They realize that the suggestions listed as ''enrichment'' are often quite good. In some instances, whole-language teachers have students select stories from the basal text as part of their literature-based reading program. If workbooks accompanying the basal texts are required, the teachers select only those pages they feel might help students become more thoughtful readers. At times, they have students work in pairs or groups to complete workbook pages, asking them to defend or justify their responses rather than simply counting them right or wrong. Other suggestions for making compromises with traditional methods and materials can be found in Chapter 2 (see pp. 28–29).

As for other language-arts areas, if whole-language teachers are required to use an English text, they proceed through it quickly. For example, they might use it only one or two days a week. This allows time for their students to engage in meaningful writing. The English text can serve as a resource as students write, revise, and edit their writing. It can also be a resource for minilessons, after which the teacher might suggest that students read the text materials. The challenge for whole-language teachers, then, is to make the language text activities meaningful to their students. Instead of asking students to copy a letter from the language text, they ask students to use the letter format in the book to write and actually send real letters to places and people for authentic purposes. If whole-language teachers are required to use a spelling text and give spelling tests, they compress the time they spend on such activities. They have students proceed through selected activities in the book on their own and give a quick spelling test on Friday covering the words in the spelling unit for that week. In this way, they meet the school's requirements by "covering" the book and they do not waste students' time.

Can teachers in departmentalized situations use whole-language approaches?

Middle grade teachers in self-contained classrooms usually make their own decisions about their schedules. Whole-language teachers in such classrooms provide a large block of time for the language arts; they do not make separate schedules for spelling, grammar, and handwriting.

Other middle grade teachers are in departmentalized situations that often resemble a high school. In these cases individual teachers have little control over the schedule. The school day is usually divided into six or seven equal or nearly equal periods, which makes it very difficult to keep language whole. Goodlad's comments (8, p. 112) about departmentalization are worth noting here:

The never-ending movement of students and teachers from class to class appears not conducive to teachers and students getting to know one another, let alone to their establishing a stable, mutually supportive relationship. Indeed, it would appear to foster casualness and neutrality in human relations . . .

For teachers in a high-school schedule situation, however, it may not be hopeless. We know teachers in departmentalized programs who use approaches with their students that are congruent with their whole-language beliefs. For example, they conduct writing workshops in the scheduled language arts or English period. We also know teachers who use students' self-selected literature as the heart of the reading program. It is not easy, but they and their students tell and show us it is time and effort well spent.

If some teacher specialization around content areas is desired, we suggest a schedule that allows for larger blocks of time. This arrangement is advocated by most middle school authorities (1). There are several variations to block scheduling, but we prefer one that keeps the number of teachers working with a group of students to a minimum. In two teacher teams we know of, one teacher has the students for a large block of time for language arts and social studies, the other has them for mathematics and science.

What about the noise level in a whole-language classroom?

Some administrators and teachers are concerned about the noise that is generated in a whole-language classroom. A great anomaly in American life is that only young people are expected to learn "on their own." In the adult world—in a business office, a legislative assembly, a scientific laboratory, or on a construction site—learning is typically a cooperative affair. Students or adults can, and should, learn from one another. Sharing ideas and exchanging points of view are essential to learning in a chemistry laboratory at DuPont or in a middle grade classroom. Teachers, therefore, must maximize the amount of social interaction between and among their students. This idea is not new. Years ago the great American philosopher and educator, John Dewey, developed it at length in such books as *Democracy and Education* (4) and *Experience and Education* (5). Were he alive today we would like to think that his eyes would light up on a visit to a whole-language classroom.

During much of the school day in whole-language classrooms, there is a learning "hum." The noise may be difficult for some teachers or administrators who believe that a good classroom environment is a perfectly quiet one. But when such skeptics observe the positive effects of social interaction on students' literacy development and attitudes, they often change their opinions and value it as much as we do.

How do whole-language teachers cope with the formal assessments of reading and writing?

Another concern of administrators is the achievement of students as measured by formal tests. Standardized and criterion-referenced tests consist of skills that do not provide an adequate profile of students' actual reading and writing abilities. Since teachers and students are often evaluated on the basis of test scores, many teachers feel compelled to drill students on the skills that will be assessed. Thus, the tests drive the curriculum. All of us must work for a change to more appropriate assessment procedures.

Meanwhile, whole-language teachers are not allowing themselves to be intimidated by these tests. They are keeping their language arts curriculum focused on meaning, not on isolated skills. Fortunately, their students score as well as and often better than those in skills-oriented classrooms.

CONCLUDING COMMENT

Professional teachers should have the power to design the curriculum in their classrooms. A professional teacher is self-directed and autonomous and, of course, competent. If teachers have the freedom to teach in ways that reflect their professional competence, teaching and learning improve.

Whole-language teachers are helping one another in support groups. Teachers Applying Whole Language (TAWL), for example, started by Ken and Yetta Goodman in Tucson, Arizona, and Dorothy Watson in Columbia, Missouri, has many local groups. There are also other less formal groups where teachers meet to share their ideas about language learning and to support one another. In addition to the support groups, formal and informal, several professional organizations provide a way for professionals to interact with and give support to one another. For example, the International Reading Association sponsors a whole-language special interest group. And the National Council of Teachers of English and the National Education Association provide ideas and support for whole-language teachers.

49

Teachers in several schools in our area have also started support groups in whole language. They meet to share ideas, discuss problems, and give one another the intellectual and moral support needed to continue improving their reading and writing programs. If you do not belong to such a group, we recommend that you join one. Or, if there is not a support group in your area, why not join hands with other interested teachers and start one? We wish you well on your journey.

Appendix A

PUBLISHERS OF STUDENTS' WRITING

Co-Ed Magazine
50 West 44th Street
New York, NY 10036
(accepts poetry)

Cricket
Box 100
LaSalle, IL 61301
(accepts poetry, stories, and drawings)

Highlights for Children
803 Church Street
Honesdale, PA 18431
(accepts poetry and stories)

Kids Magazine
P.O. Box 3041
Grand Central Station
New York, NY 10017
(accepts short stories, poetry, nonfiction)

Prairie Schooner
201 Andrews Hall
University of Nebraska
Lincoln, NE 68588
(accepts poetry)

Published Poet Newsletter
Quill Pen Publishing Company
Box 1663
Indianapolis, IN 46206
(accepts poetry)

Stone Soup
Box 83
Santa Cruz, CA 95063
(accepts stories, poetry, personal essays,
art work, and photographs)

51

Appendix B

SELECTED FAVORITE BOOKS*

Abel's Island. William Steig. New York: Farrar, 1976.

About David. Susan Beth Pheffer. New York: Delacorte, 1980.

The Adventures of Huckleberry Finn. Mark Twain. New York: Scholastic, 1983 (first published in 1884).

Anastasia Krupnik. Lois Lowry. Boston: Houghton Mifflin, 1979.

And Nobody Knew They Were There. Otto R. Salassi. New York: Greenwillow, 1984.

Anne Frank. The Diary of a Young Girl. Anne Frank. New York: Doubleday, 1946.

Anne of Green Gables. L. M. Montgomery. New York: Grosset and Dunlap, 1915.

Banner in the Sky. James Ramsey Ullman. New York. Lippincott, 1954.

Beat the Turtle Drum. Constance C. Green. New York: Viking, 1976.

Beauty: A Retelling of Beauty and the Beast. Robin McKinley. New York: Harper, 1978.

Below the Root. Zilpha Keatley Snyder. New York: Atheneum, 1975.

The Book of Three. Lloyd Alexander. New York: Holt, 1964.

Born Free: A Lioness of Two Worlds. Joy Adamson. New York: Pantheon, 1960.

Brian's Song. William Blinn. New York: Bantam, 1972.

Bridge to Terabithia. Katherine Paterson. New York: Crowell, 1977.

But We Are Not of Earth. Jean E. Karl. New York: Dutton, 1981.

---

*Although most of the authors in this list have written several other excellent books, we have given only one book for each author. Our selections range in level of difficulty and interest for middle grade students. They are books that we and the teachers with whom we work have noted that middle grade students particularly enjoy.

Caddie Woodlawn. Carol Brink. New York: Macmillan, 1936.

The Call of the Wild. Jack London. New York: Penguin, 1981 (latest printing).

Captain Grey. Avi. New York. Scholastic, 1982.

The Case of the Threatened King. Robert Newman. New York: Atheneum, 1982.

The Cat Ate My Gymsuit. Paula Danziger. New York: Dell, 1974.

Charlotte's Web. E. B. White. New York: Harper, 1952.

Close Enough to Touch. Richard Peck. New York: Delacorte, 1981.

The Creatures. John Rowe Townsend. New York: Lippincott, 1980.

Cricket in Times Square. George Selden. New York: Farrar, 1960.

The Dark Is Rising. Susan Cooper. New York: Atheneum, 1973.

A Day No Pigs Would Die. Robert Newton Peck. New York: Knopf, 1972.

Dicey's Song. Cynthia Voigt. New York: Macmillan, 1984.

Did You Carry the Flag Today, Charley? Rebecca Caudill. New York: Holt, 1971.

A Dog Called Kitty. Bill Wallace. New York: Archway, 1980.

Down a Dark Hall. Lois Duncan. Boston: Little, Brown, 1974.

The Eyes of the Killer Robot. John Bellairs. New York: Dial, 1986.

The Fledgling. Jane Langton. New York: Harper, 1980.

Freedom Train: The Story of Harriet Tubman. Dorothy Sterling. New York: Scholastic, 1987.

The Girl with the Silver Eyes. Wilo Davis Roberts. New York: Atheneum, 1980.

Hoops. Walter Dean Myers. New York: Delacorte, 1981.

House of Sixty Fathers. Meindert de Jong. New York: Harper, 1956.

How to Eat Fried Worms. Thomas Rockwell. New York: Franklin Watts, 1973.

The Incredible Journey. Sheila Burnford. Boston: Little, Brown, 1960.

The Indian in the Cupboard. Lynne Reid Banks. New York: Doubleday, 1980.

Island of the Blue Dolphins. Scott O'Dell. Boston: Houghton Mifflin, 1960.

James and the Giant Peach. Roald Dahl. New York: Knopf, 1961.

Julie of the Wolves. Jean Craighead George. New York: Harper, 1972.

The Lion, the Witch, and the Wardrobe. C. S. Lewis. New York: Macmillan, 1951.

Little House in the Big Woods. Laura Ingalls Wilder. New York: Harper, 1953.

Lord of the Flies. William Golding. New York: Putnam, 1954.

The Macmillan Book of Greek Gods and Heroes. Alice Low. New York: Macmillan, 1985.

Mama's Going to Buy You a Mockingbird. Jean Little. New York: Viking, 1984.

The Midnight Fox. Betsy C. Byars. New York: Viking, 1968.

Missing Since Monday. Ann M. Martin. New York: Holiday House, 1986.

Moon of the Three Rings. Andre Norton. New York: Viking, 1966.

Mrs. Frisby and the Rats of Nimh. Robert C. O'Brien. New York: Atheneum, 1971.

My Brother Sam Is Dead. James L. Collier and Christopher Collier. New York: Four Winds Press, 1974.

The Outsiders. S. E. Hinton. New York: Viking, 1967.

Pardon Me, You're Stepping on My Eyeball. Paul Zindel. New York: Harper, 1976.

The Planet of Junior Brown. Virginia Hamilton. New York: Macmillan, 1971.

The Red Rocking Bird. Ann Marlowe. New York: St. Martin's, 1984.

Roll of Thunder, Hear My Cry. Mildred Taylor. New York: Dial, 1976.

Savage Sam. Fred Gipson. New York: Harper, 1962.

Say Cheese. Betty Bates. New York: Holiday House, 1984.

Say Hello to the Hit Man. Jay Bennett. New York: Delacorte, 1976.

The Seance. John Lowery Nixon. San Diego: Harcourt Brace Jovanovich, 1980.

The Secret Garden. Frances Hodgson Burnett. New York: Dell, 1971 (first published in 1909).

Seven Kisses in a Row. Patricia MacLachlan. New York: Harper, 1983.

The Signs of the Beaver. Elizabeth George Speare. Boston: Houghton Mifflin, 1983.

The Slave Dancer. Paula Fox. New York: Bradbury, 1973.

The Story of My Life. Helen Keller. New York: Doubleday, 1954.

A Stranger Came Ashore. Mollie Hunter. New York: Harper, 1975.

Summer of My German Soldier. Bette Greene. New York: Dial, 1973.

Summer Switch. Mary Rodgers. New York: Harper, 1982.

Thirteen Ways to Sink a Sub. Jamie Gilson. New York: Lothrop, Lee, and Shepherd, 1954.

Tiger Eyes. Judy Blume. New York: Bradbury, 1981.

To Kill a Mockingbird. Harper Lee. New York: Harper, 1961.

Tuck Everlasting. Natalie Babbitt. New York: Farrar, 1975.

Where the Lilies Bloom. Vera Cleaver and Bill Cleaver. New York: Harper, 1969.

Where the Red Fern Grows. Wilson Rawls. New York: Doubleday, 1974.

A Wrinkle in Time. Madelyn L'Engle. New York: Farrar, 1962.

Appendix C

SELECTED POETRY COLLECTIONS

Random House Book of Poetry for Children. Collected by Jack Prelutsky. New York: Random House, 1983.

The Break Dance Kids: Poems of Sport, Motion, and Locomotion. Lillian Morrison. New York: Lothrop, Lee and Shepard, 1985.

Bronzeville Boys and Girls. Gwendolyn Brooks. New York: Harper and Row, 1956.

Hailstones and Halibut Bones. Mary O'Neill. New York: Doubleday, 1961.

Honey, I Love: And Other Love Poems. Eloise Greenfield. New York: Thomas Y. Crowell, 1972.

How Pleasant to Know Mr. Lear. Edward Lear's Selected Works by Myra Cohn Livingston. New York: Holiday House, 1982.

I Am the Darker Brother. Edited by Arnold Adoff. New York: Macmillan, 1968.

If I Were in Charge of the World. Judith Viorst. New York: Atheneum, 1981.

Kingfisher Book of Children's Poetry. Collected by Michael Rosen. London: Kingfisher Books, 1985.

A Light in the Attic. Shel Silverstein. New York: Harper, 1981.

The Malibu and Other Poems (and other poetry books by Myra Cohn Livingston). Myra Cohn Livingston. New York: Atheneum, 1972.

Monkey Puzzle and Other Poems. Myra Cohn Livingston. New York: Atheneum, 1984.

Morning Noon and Night-Time, Too (and a number of anthologies around themes as well as collections of works by specific poets). Collected by Lee Bennett Hopkins. New York: Harper, 1980.

My Black Me. Edited by Arnold Adoff. New York: E. P. Dutton, 1974.

My Daddy Is a Cool Dude. Karama Fufuka. New York: Dial Press, 1975.

New Kid on the Block. Jack Prelutsky. New York: Greenwillow Books, 1984.

On City Streets. Collected by Nancy Larrick. New York: Evans, 1968.

Rainbows Are Made: Poems by Carl Sandburg. Collected by Lee Bennett Hopkins. San Diego: Harcourt Brace Jovanovich, 1984.

Reflections on a Gift of Watermelon Pickles . . . and Other Modern Verse. Compiled by Stephen Dunning, Edward Lueders, and Hugh Smith. New York: Scholastic, 1966.

Shrieks at Midnight. Selected by Sara and John E. Brewton. New York: Crowell, 1969.

Sing a Song of Popcorn. Selected by Beatrice Shenk de Regniers and others. New York: Scholastic, 1988.

The Sky Is Full of Songs. Collected by Lee Bennett Hopkins. New York: Harper and Row, 1983.

Some Haystacks Don't Even Have Any Needles and Other Complete Modern Poems. Compiled by Stephen Dunning, Edward Lueders, and Hugh Smith. New York: Lothrop, Lee and Shepard Co., 1969.

Speak Up. David McCord. Boston: Little, Brown, 1980.

Spin a Soft Black Song. Nikki Giovanni. New York: Hill and Wang, 1985.

Where the Sidewalk Ends. Shel Silverstein. New York: Harper and Row, 1974.

Yellow Butter Purple Jelly Red Jam Black Bread. Maryann Hoberman. New York: Viking Press, 1981.

Zero Makes Me Hungry. Collected by Edward Lueders. Glenview, Ill.: Scott, Foresman, 1976.

Appendix D

SOME DISCOURSE FORMS
FOR CONTENT WRITING*

Journals and diaries
  (real or imaginary)
Biographical sketches
Anecdotes and stories:
  from experience
  as told by others
Thumbnail sketches:
  of famous people
  of places
  of content ideas
  of historical events
Guess who/what descriptions
Letters:
  personal reactions
  observations
  public/informational
  persuasive:
    to the editor
    to public officials
  to imaginary people
  from imaginary places
Requests
Applications
Memos
Resume's and summaries
Poems
Plays
Stories
Fantasy
Adventure
Science fiction
Historical stories
Dialogues and conversations
Children's books
Telegrams
Editorials
Commentaries
Responses and rebuttals
Newspaper "fillers"
Fact books or fact sheets
School newspaper stories
Stories or essays for local papers
Proposals
Case studies:
  school problems
  local issues
  national concerns
  historical problems
  scientific issues
Songs and ballads
Demonstrations
Poster displays

Reviews:
  books (including textbooks)
  films
  outside reading
  television programs
  documentaries
Historical "you are there" scenes
Scence notes:
  observations
  science notebook
  reading reports
  lab reports
Math:
  story problems
  solutions to problems
  record books
  notes and observations
Responses to literature
Utopian proposals
Practical proposals
Interviews:
  actual
  imaginary
Directions:
  how-to
  school or neighborhood guide
  survival manual
Dictionaries and lexicons
Technical reports
Future options, notes on:
  careers, employment
  school and training
  military/public service
Written debates
Taking a stand:
  school issues
  family problems
  state or national issues
  moral questions
Books and booklets
Informational monographs
Radio scripts
TV scenarios and scripts
Dramatic scripts
Notes for improvised drama
Cartoons and cartoon strips
Slide show scripts
Puzzles and word searches
Prophecy and predictions
Photos and captions
Collage, montage, mobile,
  sculpture

*Reprinted with permission from Stephen N. Tchudi and Margie C. Huerta, *Teaching Writing in the Content Areas: Middle School/Junior High*, p. 12. Washington, D.C.: National Education Association, 1983.

REFERENCES

1. Alexander, William M., and George, Paul S. *The Exemplary Middle School.* New York: Holt, 1981.

2. Atwell, Nancie. "Writing and Reading Literature from the Inside Out." *Language Arts* 61 (March 1984): 240–52.

3. Calkins, Lucy. *The Art of Teaching Writing.* Portsmouth, N.H.: Heinemann Educational Books, 1986.

4. Dewey, John. *Democracy and Education.* New York: Macmillan, 1916.

5. _____. *Experience and Education.* New York: Macmillan, 1938.

6. Fagan, William T.; Cooper, Charles R.; and Jensen, Julie M. *Measures for Research and Evaluation in the English Language Arts.* Urbana, Ill.: National Council of Teachers of English, 1975.

7. Fulwiler, Toby. "Journals Across the Disciplines." *English Journal* 69 (December 1980): 14–19.

8. Goodlad, John. *A Place Called School.* New York: McGraw-Hill, 1984.

9. Goodman, Kenneth; Smith, E. Brooks; Meredith, Robert; and Goodman, Yetta. 3d ed. *Language and Thinking in School—A Whole Language Curriculum.* New York: Richard C. Owens Publishers, 1987.

10. Goodman, Yetta, and Burke, Carolyn. *Reading Strategies: Focus on Comprehension.* New York: Richard C. Owens Publishers, 1980.

11. Goodman, Yetta; Watson, Dorothy; and Burke, Carolyn. *Reading Miscue Inventory.* New York: Richard C. Owens Publishers, 1987.

12. Graves, Donald. *Writing: Teachers and Children at Work.* Portsmouth, N.J.: Heinemann Educational Books, 1983.

13. Graves, Donald, and Hansen, Jane. "The Author's Chair." *Language Arts* 60 (February 1983): 176–83.

14. Holdaway, Don. *The Foundations of Literacy.* Portsmouth, N.H.: Heinemann Educational Books, 1979.

15. Hornsby, David, and Sukarna, Deborah. *Read On: A Conference Approach to Reading.* Portsmouth, N.H.: Heinemann Educational Books, 1986.

16. Kamii, Constance, and Randazzo, Marie. "Social Interaction and Invented Spelling." *Language Arts* 62 (February 1985): 124–33.

17. Long, Roberta; Manning, Maryann; and Manning, Gary. "One-on-One on Reading." *Teaching, K–8* 17 (February 1987): 59–62.

18. Moore, David; Moore, Susan; Cunningham, Patricia; and Cunningham, James. *Developing Readers and Writers in the Content Areas.* New York: Longman, 1986.

19. Murray, Donald. *Write to Learn.* 3d ed. New York: Holt, Rinehart, and Winston, 1987.

20. Myers, Miles. *A Procedure for Writing Assessment and Holistic Scoring.* Urbana, Ill.: National Council of Teachers of English, 1980.

21. Perret-Clermont, A. N. *Social Interaction and Cognitive Development.* London: Academic Press, 1980.

22. Piaget, Jean. *The Psychology of Intelligence.* Paterson, N.J.: Littlefield, Adams, and Co., 1963 (first published in 1947).

23. *P.S. Write Soon! All About Letters.* Urbana, Ill.: National Council of Teachers of English, 1982.

24. Rye, James. *Cloze Procedure and the Teaching of Reading.* Portsmouth, N.H.: Heinemann Educational Books, 1982.

25. Trealease, Jim. *The Read-Aloud Handbook.* New York: Penguin, 1985.

26. Vacca, Richard, and Vacca, Joanne. *Content Area Reading.* 3d ed. Glenview, Ill.: Scott, Foresman and Co., 1989.

27. Veatch, Jeanette. *Reading in the Elementary School.* New York: Richard C. Owens, 1985.

ANNOTATED BIBLIOGRAPHY

Atwell, Nancie. *In the Middle*. Upper Montclair, N.J.: Boynton/Cook Publishers, 1987.

Atwell's focus is on middle-level students. This well-written book will provide the reader with many practical ideas for creating a process-centered language arts program.

Calkins, Lucy. *The Art of Teaching Writing*. Portsmouth, N.H.: Heinemann Educational Books, 1986.

Calkins gives her views about writing in the language arts and across the curriculum. Her descriptions of writing development and suggestions for teaching writing at each grade level are especially helpful. The book reflects her excellent style as a writer, which makes the reader want to keep on reading.

Cullinan, Bernice E., ed. *Children's Literature in the Reading Program*. Newark, Del.: International Reading Association, 1987.

This is an excellent resource for guiding teachers in selecting children's books and using them with readers. The section devoted to middle-grade readers addresses multicultural issues and books and strategies for using books.

Farr, Roger. *Reading: Trends and Challenges*. 2d ed. Washington, D.C.: National Education Association, 1986.

Farr gives an excellent and brief review of selected reading research and the status of reading in the United States. He emphasizes the idea that the teacher is still the key to reading instruction.

Goodman, Kenneth. *What's Whole in Whole Language*. Portsmouth, N.H.: Heinemann Educational Books, 1986.

This easy-to-read book describing the whole-language movement addresses language development and reading and writing development. It also provides suggestions for helping children become literate, using examples of successful whole-language programs.

Goodman, Kenneth; Smith, E. Brooks; Meredith, Robert; and Goodman, Yetta. *Language and Thinking in School—A Whole Language Curriculum*. 3d ed. New York: Richard C. Owens Publishers, 1987.

The authors discuss the relationships among language, thought processes, and education, and provide ways to build and assess curriculum and instruction. They emphasize the fact that teachers need a base of knowledge and theory in order to help their students develop. The book reflects the extensive developments that have occurred in language and thinking during the last decade. It is essential reading for those interested in a "scientific" view of education.

Goodman, Kenneth; Goodman, Yetta; and Hood, Wendy, eds. *The Whole Language Evaluation Book*. Portsmouth, N.H.: Heinemann Educational Books, 1989.

This collection of articles written by classroom teachers provides ideas for strategies for evaluating students' reading and writing. Whole-language teachers will find the book a valuable resource for evaluation strategies that are consistent with whole-language beliefs.

Hansen, Jane. *When Writers Read*. Portsmouth, N.H.: Heinemann Educational Books, 1987.

Hansen makes the connections between reading and writing instruction. She provides ideas that will help teachers become process-centered in the teaching of reading.

Harste, Jerome C., and Short, Kathy G., with Carolyn Burke. *Creating Classrooms for Authors*. Portsmouth, N.H.: Heinemann Educational Books, 1988.

Teachers will find this book a very helpful source of practical suggestions for organizing a process-centered classroom and for developing process reading and writing activities. In addition to its practical nature, a strong theoretical frame is apparent.

Hobson, Eric, and Shuman, R. Baird. *Reading and Writing in High Schools: A Whole-Language Approach*. Washington, D.C.: National Education Association, 1990.

As Hobson and Shuman point out, all the arts of communication overlap and interact. Consequently, their focus is on the skills of decoding (reading and listening) and encoding (writing and speaking). In addition to providing the theoretical basis for the whole-language approach, they also suggest exercises that teachers can adapt to their own classroom situations.

Holdaway, Don. *Stability and Change in Literacy Learning*. Portsmouth, N.H.: Heinemann Educational Books, 1984.

Using a developmental perspective, Holdaway gives clear and sound ideas for teaching young children to read and write. He includes a helpful discussion about shared book experiences.

Hornsby, David, and Sukarna, Deborah. *Read On: A Conference Approach to Reading*. Portsmouth, N.H.: Heinemann Educational Books, 1986.

This book gives many practical suggestions for a literature-based reading program. Especially helpful are the ideas for individual and small-group reading conferences.

Manning, Gary and Manning, Maryann, eds. *Whole Language: Beliefs and Practices, K-8*. Washington, D.C.: National Education Association, 1989.

This anthology deals with whole-language theory and teaching practices that are congruent with such theory. It includes contributions by such well-known whole-language authorities as Kenneth and Yetta Goodman, Dorothy Watson, and Carole Edelsky.

Newkirk, Thomas, and Atwell, Nancie, eds. *Understanding Writing*. Chelmsford, Mass.: Northeast Regional Exchange, 1982.

This collection deals with beginning writing, conferences, writing and reading relationships, and assessment. It provides insights about the ways children learn to read and write, and how classroom teachers can help them.

Newman, Judith M., ed. *Whole Language—Theory in Use*. Portsmouth, N.H.: Heinemann Educational Books, 1985.

This publication provides specific ideas for teaching reading and writing from a whole-language perspective and for creating meaningful literacy environments in which students are active in their own learning. Specific areas addressed include children's books, journal writing, spelling, and conferencing.

Rhodes, Lynn K., and Dudley-Marling, Curt. *Readers and Writers with a Difference: A Holistic Approach to Teaching Learning-Disabled and Remedial Students.* Portsmouth, N.H.: Heinemann Educational Books, 1988.

Rhodes and Dudley-Marling give an excellent holistic perspective on reading and writing for teachers who work with learning-disabled students. They provide specific strategies for helping students.

Tchudi, Stephen N. and Huerta, Margie C. *Teaching Writing in the Content Areas: Middle School/Junior High.* Washington, D.C.: National Education Association, 1983.

Tchudi and Huerta provide ideas for content area writing, including procedures for lesson plans, model units, topics, and evaluation and grading. They emphasize the importance of keeping content at the center of the writing process and give suggestions for doing so.

Thaiss, Christopher. *Language Across the Curriculum in the Elementary Grades.* Urbana, Ill.: National Council of Teachers of English, 1986.

Thaiss reviews research findings related to the language-across-the-curriculum approach. He shows how to use speaking, writing, listening, and reading to teach content. Suggested activities include logs, journals, games, and small-group discussion.

Watson, Dorothy, ed. *Ideas and Insights: Language Arts in the Elementary School.* Urbana, Ill: National Council of Teachers of English, 1987.

This book is filled with activities that reflect a whole-language view. Leland Jacobs, Kenneth Goodman, and Donald Graves provide good insights in the introductory section. All five sections of the book contain many activities from a large number of contributors.